U.S. Department of Justice
Office of Justice Programs
810 Seventh Street NW.
Washington, DC 20531

Eric H. Holder, Jr.
Attorney General

Mary Lou Leary
Acting Assistant Attorney General

Melodee Hanes
Acting Administrator
Office of Juvenile Justice and Delinquency Prevention

Office of Justice Programs
Innovation • Partnerships • Safer Neighborhoods
www.ojp.usdoj.gov

Office of Juvenile Justice and Delinquency Prevention
www.ojjdp.gov

The Office of Juvenile Justice and Delinquency Prevention is a component of the Office of Justice Programs, which also includes the Bureau of Justice Assistance; the Bureau of Justice Statistics; the National Institute of Justice; the Office for Victims of Crime; and the Office of Sex Offender Sentencing, Monitoring, Apprehending, Registering, and Tracking.

AMBER Alert
Best Practices

May 2012
NCJ 232271

America's Missing:
Broadcast Emergency Response

This document was prepared under cooperative agreement number 2008–MC–CX–K028 from the Office of Juvenile Justice and Delinquency Prevention (OJJDP), U.S. Department of Justice. Points of view or opinions expressed in this document are those of the authors and do not necessarily represent the official position or policies of OJJDP or the U.S. Department of Justice.

Message From Acting Assistant Attorney General Mary Lou Leary

Few events can galvanize a community to action like the news that a child has been forcibly taken from his or her home or family. Fortunately, we have AMBER Alert, a program that helps communities coordinate their efforts to find, rescue, and return abducted children to their families.

Over the past decade and a half, AMBER Alert has grown from a single local program in Arlington, TX, into a network of state, local, regional, tribal, and territorial plans throughout the United States and Canada. AMBER Alert continues to expand, as Mexico and other countries have launched their own AMBER Alert or similar plans. This sustained growth is heartening.

As National AMBER Alert Coordinator, I am concerned about how we can improve the program. Each AMBER Alert plan is a complex partnership involving law enforcement, broadcasters, transportation agencies, the wireless industry, and the community. We continually ask these stakeholders to identify which strategies and practices have enhanced their ability to find and safely recover abducted children.

This guide is a compilation of everything that our AMBER Alert partners have told us constitutes an effective and efficient program. The true testimony to just how effective AMBER Alert has become can be found in the stories of each of the hundreds of abducted children who have been rescued and safely returned to their families as a result of this program.

The AMBER Alert Program is a crucial component of a larger, comprehensive effort to respond to child abduction. As we continue to enhance and improve the program, we come closer to realizing our goal of keeping our nation's children safe.

Mary Lou Leary
Acting Assistant Attorney General
National AMBER Alert Coordinator

Foreword

The first few minutes and hours after a child has been abducted are critical to any search and rescue effort. They often can mean the difference between a happy reunion between parents and child and missed opportunities and regret. At these crucial moments, everyone involved in the search and rescue effort must understand how the entire process works and his or her role in the effort. This guide, which spells out roles and responsibilities and the progression of events in a well-coordinated AMBER Alert process, was created to support and improve national, state, regional, and local responses to child abductions.

Over the past decade, as AMBER Alert has expanded into a nationwide program, we at the Office of Justice Programs and the Office of Juvenile Justice and Delinquency Prevention have worked hard to identify what works and how we can improve the process of issuing an alert and coordinating public input into the search. We have sought out the many AMBER Alert stakeholders for their expertise and insights into how to enhance the process.

Our partners have told us a great deal about what works and what issues must be considered to develop an effective AMBER Alert plan. This publication encapsulates the knowledge and expertise that our partners have shared with us. It provides a general overview of each discipline's responsibilities when an AMBER Alert has been issued and recommends practices to improve the response to cases of missing or abducted children.

We have made tremendous progress since 1996, when the first AMBER Alert plan was launched. However, as with any major initiative that brings together many agencies and organizations, we must remain vigilant and find ways to improve our understanding of how each stakeholder's role and responsibility fits into the overall collaboration.

The stakes are high because the safety and welfare of our children are in the balance. This guide will help states and communities more effectively execute and coordinate their response when their children need them the most.

Melodee Hanes

Melodee Hanes
Acting Administrator
Office of Juvenile Justice and Delinquency Prevention

Acknowledgments

The development of the AMBER Alert Program has been perhaps the most significant operational step taken in several decades to recover missing, endangered, and abducted children in the United States. Creating a national missing child alert system involving multiple partners in the private and public sectors as well as the general public has necessarily required significant leadership, untiring commitment, and relentless dedication by many partners to advance the safeguards of America's missing children.

The Office of Juvenile Justice and Delinquency Prevention (OJJDP) owes its sincere gratitude to the team of professionals from Fox Valley Technical College, which delivers the AMBER Alert Training and Technical Assistance Program; First Pic, Inc.; and Ronald C. Laney, former Senior Advisor to the Administrator and Associate Administrator of the Child Protection Division at OJJDP.

The following individuals are recognized for their contributions to this document.

Program Director

Phil Keith, AMBER Alert Training and Technical Assistance Program

Primary Author

Donna Uzzell, Director, Criminal Justice Information Systems, Florida Department of Law Enforcement

Contributors

Byron Fassett, Sergeant, Child Exploitation Squad, Dallas (TX) Police Department

Robert Hoever, Associate Director of Special Projects and Forensic Services, National Center for Missing & Exploited Children

Brian Killacky, Supervisor, Investigations Bureau, Office of the State's Attorney of Cook County, IL

Paul Murphy, Director of Communications & Policy, Utah Attorney General's Office

Gus Paidousis, Deputy Chief, Knoxville (TN) Police Department

Floy Turner, Consultant, Fox Valley Technical College

Jim Walters, Liaison for Tribal and Border Initiatives, AMBER Alert Training and Technical Assistance Program

OJJDP acknowledges key partners from the media; the broadcast industry; the wireless industry; state, local, regional, and tribal AMBER Alert Coordinators; state missing children clearinghouses; the National Center for Missing & Exploited Children; the Surviving Parents Coalition; and other private- and public-sector partners that have championed the efforts through their many strategic and operational efforts. Collectively, these partnerships, as well as leaders at various levels of government and in the private sector, have played a critical role in improving the AMBER Alert Program and recovering America's missing, endangered, and abducted children.

Contents

Introduction

The AMBER (America's Missing: Broadcast Emergency Response) Alert Program began following the 1996 abduction and murder of 9-year-old Amber Hagerman in Arlington, TX. In response to this tragedy, representatives from law enforcement and the local media joined forces to develop and implement a groundbreaking series of protocols to be followed in the event of a child abduction. The program has since expanded to include 133 state, local, regional, tribal, and territorial plans in the United States and Canada. As of March 2012, AMBER Alerts helped directly in the safe recovery of 572 children in the United States.[1]

The AMBER Alert Program is a voluntary partnership involving law enforcement, broadcasters, transportation agencies, and the wireless industry. It is designed to disseminate timely, accurate information about abducted children, the suspected abductor(s), and the vehicle(s) used in the commission of the crime. During an AMBER Alert, an urgent news bulletin is broadcast over the airwaves and via text messages as well as on highway alert signs to enlist the aid of the public in finding an abducted child and stopping the perpetrator.

Participants and subject-matter experts attending a federally sponsored national AMBER Alert conference identified emerging practices that have enhanced the ability of law enforcement, other stakeholders, and partners to safely recover missing and abducted children. This report provides a "what works" approach based on what was garnered during the conference as well as the experience and knowledge gained since the inception of the first AMBER Alert plan. It offers the field additional information about effective and promising practices and is designed for interpretation at the state and local levels in a manner that allows teams to consider their resource limitations and diverse demographic and geographic needs.

In addition, because the AMBER Alert Program is a collaborative effort involving multiple agencies, the public, and the media, the report provides a general overview of each discipline's responsibilities along with suggested practices to improve the approach to responding to cases of missing or abducted children.

Significant progress has been made since 1996; however, as with any major multiagency initiative, all program partners and stakeholders must remain vigilant and work collaboratively to improve their understanding of the roles and responsibilities of every agency and organization involved in the program. Partners must be open-minded when communicating with each other and always strive to meet the ultimate goal—keeping our children safe.

Chapter I. Overview of Existing Research

Before entering into a review of the AMBER Alert Program, it is important to have a clear picture of the nature and scope of the problem of missing and exploited children. A number of studies have been conducted to provide a better understanding and definition of who missing children are, what happens to them when they are taken, and the actions required to find them.

The Missing Children's Assistance Act of 1984[2] provides practitioners, policymakers, and researchers with useful data that define (1) the severity of abductions and (2) the characteristics of children who are abducted, missing from their caretakers, or sexually exploited. In addition, the Act requires the Administrator of the Office of Juvenile Justice and Delinquency Prevention (OJJDP) to "periodically conduct national incidence studies to determine for a given year the actual number of children reported missing each year, the number of children who are victims of abduction by strangers, the number of children who are the victims of parental kidnappings, and the number of children who are recovered each year."[3] Findings from two of those studies, the Case Management for Missing Children Homicide Investigation[4] and the National Incidence Studies of Missing, Abducted, Runaway, and Thrownaway Children (NISMART), underscore the necessity of the AMBER Alert Program and are discussed below.

Case Management for Missing Children Homicide Investigation

This 3-year study, the first of its kind, was funded by OJJDP and conducted by the Washington State Attorney General's Office. The study area covered 44 states and included both large and small law enforcement agencies in urban, suburban, and rural areas. Researchers examined 833 cases (27.4 percent unsolved) with 621 victims (74 percent female and 26 percent male) and 419 murderers.

The study findings support the need for a rapid, comprehensive community response to missing children cases. Timing is critical when reporting that a child is missing. In 43 percent of the cases in which a child was killed, more than 2 hours passed between the time the victim was known to be missing and the time a report was made to law enforcement. In 76 percent of those cases, the victims were dead within 3 hours of the abduction. For more detailed information about these findings, see www.missingkids.com/en_US/documents/homicide_missing.pdf.

National Incidence Studies of Missing, Abducted, Runaway, and Thrownaway Children

The National Incidence Studies of Missing, Abducted, Runaway, and Thrownaway Children, commonly referred to as NISMART–1[5] (1984) and NISMART–2[6] (1999), were conducted as a component of ongoing data collection by the Department of Justice and its contracted partners.

NISMART identified several categories of missing children, including nonfamily abductions, stereotypical kidnapping,[7] family abductions, runaway/thrownaway and lost children, and injured or otherwise missing children. It is important to note that the data collected and reported in both NISMART studies are research data that represent a dramatic example of the incredibly high numbers of children who go missing each year.

It is estimated that more than 1.3 million children go missing each year. Although most of these children return home, this number underscores the significance of the problem and mandates the effective and efficient involvement of law enforcement. Information and statistics from the NISMART–2 study can be found at www.ncjrs.gov/pdffiles1/ojjdp/196469.pdf.

Chapter 2. Development of the AMBER Alert Network

Creating and maintaining an effective AMBER Alert network is essential for continued success in recovering missing, endangered, and abducted children.

The PROTECT Act

On April 30, 2003, President George W. Bush signed into law the Prosecutorial Remedies and Other Tools to End the Exploitation of Children Today (PROTECT) Act,[8] which comprehensively strengthened law enforcement's ability to prevent, investigate, prosecute, and punish violent crimes committed against children. The Act reinforced the need for every state to have a plan to notify the public and law enforcement of child abductions and to coordinate search efforts for missing children, and it provided funding and resources to encourage states to implement strategies that would streamline the approach to safely recovering missing and abducted children.

In addition, the Act created a level of national leadership by designating the Assistant Attorney General for the Office of Justice Programs (OJP) to serve in the position of a National AMBER Alert Coordinator to assist states in the development of those plans and to provide guidance on the issuance and dissemination of AMBER Alerts. Since the adoption of the AMBER Alert Program by the U.S. Department of Justice, all 50 states, Puerto Rico, the Virgin Islands, and the District of Columbia have established and maintained coordinated AMBER Alert plans. In addition, more than 80 local, regional, and tribal AMBER Alert plans have been established.

Components of a Comprehensive Child Recovery Strategy

Although an AMBER Alert plan is critical to safely recovering abducted children, it should be considered as one tool in a larger, comprehensive approach to recovering abducted children. A significant strategy of OJP's approach to creating a systematic response is to expand the capacities and capabilities of state and local law enforcement officials and other child protection professionals to respond to such incidents. Figure 1 (page 6) depicts the policy and program components that need to be in place to create or enhance an AMBER Alert plan.

Other important components of an effective strategy include:

Stakeholders and Partners

Identifying key stakeholders and partners who will play a primary role in the dissemination of an alert is central to an effective, robust AMBER Alert system. The plan's success ultimately rests on the involvement of critical stakeholders and partners who actively participate in the monitoring, planning, and development of an effective and seamless missing child alert system.

Representatives from law enforcement, the media, and departments of transportation are the most important AMBER Alert stakeholders. Through media outlets and roadway message signs, critical timely information is disseminated to the public. Other stakeholders, including emergency–911 (E–911) centers, Attorney Generals' offices, emergency management personnel, and community-based organizations, also play an important role in the dissemination of information to the public. Organizations and agencies, such as lottery commissions, cell phone and paging companies, Internet service providers, and outdoor advertising companies, also have become active partners in disseminating information about AMBER Alerts.

State and local community leaders participate in the AMBER Alert Program by setting policies, establishing criteria, and providing oversight. Careful and continuous information sharing

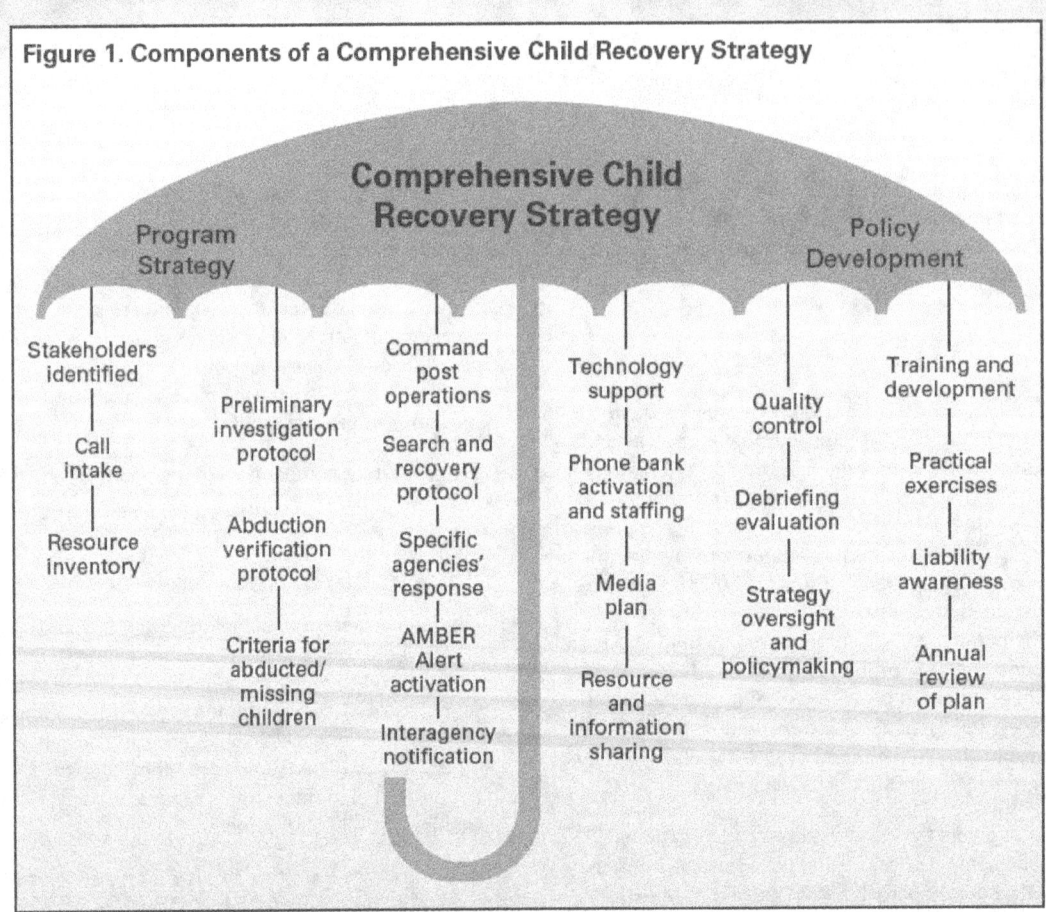

Figure 1. Components of a Comprehensive Child Recovery Strategy

Comprehensive Child Recovery Strategy

Program Strategy

Policy Development

Stakeholders identified

Call intake

Resource inventory

Preliminary investigation protocol

Abduction verification protocol

Criteria for abducted/ missing children

Command post operations

Search and recovery protocol

Specific agencies' response

AMBER Alert activation

Interagency notification

Technology support

Phone bank activation and staffing

Media plan

Resource and information sharing

Quality control

Debriefing evaluation

Strategy oversight and policymaking

Training and development

Practical exercises

Liability awareness

Annual review of plan

through regular meetings and ongoing briefings is important for program monitoring and evaluation. All stakeholders and partners should be convened and given specific tasks so they can become actively engaged in the plan. Although law enforcement agencies typically take the lead role in the plan, the AMBER Alert system may require changes in E–911 centers and state department of transportation messaging systems. Therefore, the formation and fostering of cooperative bridges should be a continuing focus in the process to enhance partnerships and create solid program foundations.

AMBER Alert Criteria for Missing and Abducted Children

Every successful AMBER Alert plan contains clearly defined activation criteria. The following guidance is designed to achieve a uniform, interoperable network of plans across the country and to minimize potentially deadly delays because of confusion among jurisdictions with varying alert criteria. OJP developed the information with input from AMBER Alert stakeholders around the country. More information on the AMBER Alert criteria is available at www.amberalert.gov.

Abduction verification protocol. AMBER Alert plans require law enforcement to confirm an abduction before issuing an alert. This is essential when determining the level of risk to the child. Clearly, stranger abductions are the most dangerous to children and thus are primary to the mission of an AMBER Alert. However, family abductions, especially where domestic violence is a factor, should also be considered potentially dangerous to the safety of the child or children involved. In some family abduction cases, the issuance of an AMBER Alert or Endangered Missing Advisory may be the best recourse to assist in the safe recovery of the child. Allowing activations in the absence of significant information that an abduction has occurred could lead to abuse of the system and ultimately weaken its effectiveness. At the same time, each case must be appraised on its own merits, and a judgment call must be made quickly. Law enforcement must understand that a "best judgment" approach, based on the evidence, is appropriate and necessary.

Risk of serious bodily injury or death. Plans require a child to be at risk for serious bodily injury or death before an alert can be issued. This criterion is clearly related to law enforcement's recognition that stranger abductions represent the greatest danger to children. The need for timely, accurate information based on strict and clearly understood criteria is critical, again keeping in mind the best judgment approach.

Sufficient descriptive information. For an AMBER Alert to be effective in recovering a missing child, the law enforcement agency must have enough information to believe that an immediate broadcast to the public will enhance the efforts of law enforcement to locate the child and apprehend the suspect. This element requires as much descriptive information as possible about the abducted child, the abduction, the suspect, and the suspect's vehicle. Many plans allow for the issuance of an AMBER Alert without specific information on the abductor or a vehicle, but they may not activate road sign messaging systems unless vehicle information is known.

Age of child. Every state has adopted the "age 17 or younger" standard or, at a minimum, has agreed to honor any other state's request to issue an AMBER Alert even if the case does not meet the responding state's age criterion, as long as it meets the age criterion of the requesting state. Most AMBER Alert plans call for activation of an alert for children under a certain age; however, the age can vary according to the specific plan—ages include 10, 12, 14, 15, and 16. Differences in age requirements create confusion when an activation requires multiple alerts across several states and jurisdictions.

National Crime Information Center data entry. Data regarding the AMBER Alert should be entered into the National Crime Information Center (NCIC) system immediately, including a description of the circumstances surrounding the abduction, and the case should be flagged as a "child abduction." Some plans do not mandate entry of the data into NCIC, but this omission undermines the mission of the AMBER Alert initiative. The notation on the entry should be sufficient to explain the circumstances surrounding the disappearance of the child. Entry of the alert data into NCIC expands the search for an abducted child from a state, local, or regional level to a national level. This is a critical element of any effective AMBER Alert plan.

Department of Justice–Recommended Criteria for Activating an Alert

+ Law enforcement believes an abduction has occurred.

+ Law enforcement believes the child is in imminent danger of serious bodily injury or death.

+ Sufficient descriptive information about the victim, the suspect, and the abduction exists for law enforcement to issue an AMBER Alert.

+ The child is 17 years old or younger.

+ The child's name and other critical information, including the "child abduction" flag, have been entered into the National Crime Information Center system.

Chapter 3. The Role of Law Enforcement

As first responders in a missing child investigation, local law enforcement plays a critical role in AMBER Alert plans. The AMBER Alert system is useful only when agencies know how and when to activate an alert. Agency policies and procedures should clearly indicate the investigative response to a missing child, and this response should include the procedures and authority to request an AMBER Alert. The following information was developed by subject-matter experts who have been active in AMBER Alert programs throughout the country. It includes suggested practices in some key areas of the agency response, such as establishing phone banks, the initial response, search and rescue efforts, the use of volunteers, and officers' interactions with family members.

Call Takers

The following findings from the Case Management for Missing Children Homicide Investigation study (see chapter 1, Overview of Existing Research) highlight the necessity of an immediate response in missing child cases. Of the abducted children who were killed:

✦ Forty-four percent were killed within the first hour.

✦ Seventy-four percent were killed within the first 3 hours.

✦ Ninety-one percent were killed within the first 24 hours.

Resources: Best Practices for Call Takers

The National Center for Missing & Exploited Children's (NCMEC's) *Standard for Public Safety Telecommunicators When Responding to Calls of Missing, Abducted, and Sexually Exploited Children* (www.missingkids.com/en_US/documents/911standards.pdf) is designed to assist public safety telecommunications supervisors in defining policies, operational procedures, and training curriculums to promote an effective response to handling missing child incidents. The document outlines best practices from the initial call intake through the first onscene response and subsequent data intake. To promote alignment between communications and field operations, the standard should be used in conjunction with NCMEC's *Missing and Abducted Children: A Law Enforcement Guide to Case Investigation and Program Management* (available at www.missingkids.com).

Developed to assist call takers in applying the standard, the *Checklist for Public-Safety Telecommunicators When Responding to Calls Pertaining to Missing, Abducted, and Sexually Exploited Children* (www.missingkids.com/en_US/publications/NC200.pdf) outlines the important role of the telecommunicator as first responder, sets forth step-by-step call-intake protocols specific to each type of incident—abduction; lost, injured, or otherwise missing; runaway or thrownaway—and provides information regarding around-the-clock resources and support.

The AMBER Alert Training and Technical Assistance Program's online course, Public Safety Telecommunications Best Practices for Missing and Abducted Children, supports the standard and reinforces call takers' incorporation of both the standard and call-handling checklists into their existing operations. The program strengthens call takers' understanding of the nature of and response to the problem of missing, abducted, and sexually exploited children, which will bolster their capacity to respond effectively to every call concerning the welfare of a child. Visit www.amber-net.org and click on the "Distance Learning" tab for more information.

Reports of missing and abducted children may be among the most difficult, challenging, and emotionally charged cases that a call taker will experience. Each stage of the case, from the initial call through recovery, forms a critical component of a thorough child-recovery response. Public safety agencies must provide their staff with the tools and training that will enable them to act quickly and decisively when confronted with reports of missing and abducted children. An immediate and comprehensive response enhances the likelihood of accumulating evidence or information that might otherwise be lost during the critical early stages of an investigation.

Initial Response

The investigation begins once the call is received. The lead law enforcement agency will start the investigative process by verifying and recording pertinent information. The information gathered during the preliminary investigation will help law enforcement officials decide whether an AMBER Alert should be issued or if the case can be resolved through other methods available to the department, such as a local child alert.

Resource: Online Training for First Responders

The AMBER Alert Technical Assistance and Training Program has developed an online course to provide law enforcement officers responsible for patrol and first-response duties with the tools and training that promote a swift and decisive response in the critical early stages of incidents involving missing and abducted children. This training can be accessed at www.amber-net.org under the "Distance Learning" tab.

Preliminary Investigation

To activate an AMBER Alert, the responding agency must be confident that an abduction has occurred, that the criteria for activation have been met, and that the local agency has ruled out any other possibilities for the child's disappearance. Since time is of the essence in such situations, as much information as possible must be collected at the start of the investigation; however, this must be balanced by the need to activate the alert as quickly as possible.

During the preliminary investigation, officers should obtain the following information about the missing child:

+ Name, including nicknames.

+ Date of birth.

+ Identifying marks, such as birthmarks, moles, tattoos, and scars.

+ Height and weight.

+ Gender.

+ Race.

+ Current hair color and true or natural hair color.

+ Eye color.

+ Prosthetics, surgical implants, or cosmetic implants.

+ Physical anomalies.

+ Blood type, if known.

+ Any medications the missing child is taking or needs to take.

+ Social Security number, if known.

+ A recent photograph, if available.

+ A description of the clothing the child was believed to be wearing at the time of the disappearance.

+ A description of notable items that the child may be carrying.

- Information about the child's electronic communications, such as a cell phone number; e-mail address; MySpace, Facebook, or other social networking page; and screen names.

- Reasons why the reporting person believes the child is missing.

- Name and location of the child's school.

- Name and location of the child's dentist and primary care physician, if known.

- Any circumstances that may indicate the disappearance was not voluntary and the child may be in imminent danger.

Investigators should obtain the following information about the abductor, if known:

- Name.

- Relationship to the missing child.

- Physical description.

- Date of birth.

- Identifying marks, such as birthmarks, moles, tattoos, and scars.

- Description of possible means of transportation, such as the make, model, color, license plate number, and vehicle identification number of a motor vehicle.

- Associates.

- Any other information that can help locate the missing child.

Entry Into the National Crime Information Center Database

As soon as it has been determined that the child is missing and sufficient information is obtained, the agency should enter the information into the Federal Bureau of Investigation's (FBI's) National

Resource: Checklist for First Responders

The National Center for Missing & Exploited Children (NCMEC) has developed the *Investigative Checklist for First Responders*, which is adapted from and is a supplement to *Missing and Abducted Children: A Law Enforcement Guide to Case Investigation and Program Management*. To request a free copy or to obtain technical assistance for specific cases, call NCMEC at 800–THE–LOST (800–843–5678) or go to www.ncmecpublications.org.

Crime Information Center (NCIC) database. Section 104 of the Adam Walsh Child Protection and Safety Act of 2006 amended the reporting requirement set forth in Section 3702 of the Crime Control Act of 1990 (42 U.S.C. 5780) by replacing "immediately" with "within 2 hours of receipt." The FBI guidelines further define the entry criteria as "2 hours after enough information has been obtained to enable the entry into NCIC." The appropriate flag should be set to indicate either Child Abduction (CA) or AMBER Alert (AA). The entry should include as much information as the responding officer can provide, including the following:

- A photo of the child.

- Details of any vehicle associated with the case.

- Information about a warrant for the abductor's arrest, if one has been issued.

It is very important to link the information above to the missing child entry; the agency should use the "miscellaneous" field to note any information that cannot be entered into the prescribed fields. The investigator should reexamine the entry within 24 hours to ensure its accuracy and to add any additional information that may be obtained during the investigation.

Criteria for Adding Persons With Information

NCIC has added a searchable "Persons With Information" field. This enhancement to the Missing Person File allows the details of a person who may have information about or is possibly connected to the missing child to be added and linked to the record when a warrant has not been issued. The person must have been identified to the public, either through an AMBER Alert or other notification; must be believed to have relevant information that could aid in the location of the child; and cannot be located, with time being of the essence. Each state must ensure such programming is available to local agencies through an interface.

For questions about entering a missing person's details into NCIC, to obtain the FBI's *Data Collection Entry Guide for Missing Persons,* or for more information on "Persons With Information," contact NCIC at 304–625–3000.

Dissemination of the Alert to the Public

Public participation is a key component in the success of the AMBER Alert. The public becomes the eyes and ears of law enforcement in the search for the child. To that end, law enforcement must be diligent in ensuring that photos and videos of the child are widely distributed to and viewed by as many people as possible.

Posters

The most common way for law enforcement to disseminate an alert is to create a missing child poster or flier and to develop a distribution program. Posters and/or fliers can be made on most computer word processing programs. State clearinghouses and the National Center for Missing & Exploited Children can also assist agencies in producing a poster and/or flier and can aid in widespread distribution.

Web Sites

Maintaining a Web site can be difficult and resource intensive; however, a Web site can reach many people. If it is maintained and updated continuously, AMBER Alert participants and the media can monitor it for the latest information. Really Simple Syndication (RSS) feeds may be considered to enhance notification. Agencies should consider posting active AMBER Alerts on their homepage and requesting that other government and private entities link to it.

Social Media

Many agencies are using social media to solve crimes. Law enforcement has taken to sites such as Facebook to interact with members of the public within and outside their jurisdiction and are using this tool to aid in a variety of criminal investigations and increase community awareness. In a missing child case, social media is yet another way to broadcast information and photos that could make a difference in the recovery of the child.

Resource: Facebook's AMBER Alert Pages

In 2011, the Department of Justice and the National Center for Missing & Exploited Children teamed up with Facebook, the social networking Web site, to enable millions of Facebook users across the country to receive AMBER Alerts via their accounts (Facebook has more than half a billion users worldwide). Facebook users in the 50 states, the District of Columbia, Puerto Rico, and the U.S. Virgin Islands can sign up to receive AMBER Alerts for their region. Facebook's AMBER Alert pages contain no advertising, and users cannot post comments on the pages. This ensures that the information about the AMBER Alert being shared by users comes directly from the law enforcement agency that issued the alert. Once the alert is canceled, Facebook removes the post from all sites so users will not search for a child who has already been found.

Operating and Staffing Phone Banks

Once an AMBER Alert has been issued, its success depends on the ability of law enforcement agencies to receive, process, and prioritize leads and tips without dropping calls. Phone banks, therefore, are vital to the successful recovery of a missing child. A series of activities should be performed to ensure the effective operation of a phone bank system. These activities include establishing regional phone banks, local 911 numbers, toll-free numbers, phone stacking systems, and nonemergency numbers; securing relief personnel; providing standardized training; and creating a plan to contact other agencies for additional support.

Proper staffing and supervision structures must be in place to ensure effective management, operation, and monitoring of the system. Phone banks should be staffed by specially trained personnel who have scripted questions, and a well-defined, automated, leads tracking or case management system should be established. This ensures proper prioritization and response to every call. Although volunteers have been used for this task, doing so is not as effective as using experienced call takers. Whenever possible, seasoned police officers who are familiar with the investigation should prioritize all leads. This will allow for a more timely response to critical leads.

Phone recording to capture all conversations and rollover capabilities to avoid dropped calls should be used to ensure that all calls are answered. Coordination of 911 centers will ensure that all calls relating to the child abduction are routed to the agency managing the phone bank. In addition, private corporations, system providers, cell phone and paging companies, and related groups should be involved in the planning and development stages of the AMBER Alert system to address and discuss any potential issues relating to phone bank implementation and use. Methods for obtaining additional resources, including resource sharing and private vendor assistance, should be explored to support the enhancements to the phone bank system.

Child Abduction Response Teams

Like an AMBER Alert, a Child Abduction Response Team (CART) is a tool that agencies can employ in an abduction incident or in situations where a child is missing and believed to be in danger. A CART is a multiagency, often multijurisdictional composite of community professionals who are trained and equipped to respond in the search and recovery of an abducted or endangered child. The CART strategy incorporates three elements: trained individuals with established roles and assignments, a readymade list of equipment that is

Resources: Incident-Management Tools

The following secure, Web-based tools are available to law enforcement agencies to help organize an agency's activities during the search:

The Simple Leads Management System

Simple Leads is an easily navigable tracking system that the National Center for Missing & Exploited Children developed that can be downloaded from www.missingkids.com/lawenforcement. Click on "Links, Lists and Tools," then "Simple Leads Management System."

The Virtual Command Center

The Federal Bureau of Investigation's (FBI's) Virtual Command Center (VCC) is an information sharing and crisis management tool that allows law enforcement access to a secure Internet command center. It can be used to submit and view information, intelligence, maps, and other essential documents from local and remote sites. VCC has been used to manage law enforcement activities during major events, such as the 2009 presidential inauguration and major sporting events, as well as numerous kidnapping cases and natural disaster command activities throughout the nation. Users of VCC include the Bureau of Alcohol, Tobacco, Firearms & Explosives; the San Francisco Police Department; the Denver Police Department; and the Tennessee Bureau of Investigation. To learn more about VCC and other tools that the FBI offers, such as the Operational Response and Investigative Online Network, e-mail vccleosupport@leo.gov.

available to aid in the search, and a network of nontraditional community resources that the team can tap into to assist in the investigation. If an agency participates in or has access to a CART, it should consider requesting activation of the CART to assist in the multitude of tasks that will need to be accomplished during the investigation, such as conducting a neighborhood canvass, accounting for sex offenders in the area, and following up on leads generated by the alert. More than 200 CARTs representing 45 states, the District of Columbia, Puerto Rico, the Bahamas, and Canada have received training through the Office of Juvenile Justice and Delinquency Prevention's AMBER Alert Training and Technical Assistance Program. For more information about CART training or establishing a local CART, visit https://www.thecjportal.org/AmberAlert/Courses/Onsite. Choose "Onsite" and then "Child Abduction Response Team."

Search and Recovery Efforts

The vast majority of law enforcement agencies have no established plan or procedure for conducting a canvass or search as part of a missing child investigation. Analysis of canvass and search operations reveals a number of serious problems that have occurred during major investigations: missed witnesses; missed, damaged, or destroyed physical evidence; poor documentation; contact of suspects without officer knowledge; and difficulty in obtaining feedback from canvassers. Additional pitfalls include delays in initiating formal search activities, ambiguous authority, inadequate use of specialized resources, poor interagency communications, unplanned media relations, and inability to deal with unanticipated volunteer response.

The importance of conducting a thorough, organized neighborhood canvass—using only trained professionals with scripted questions—cannot be overemphasized. Practitioners recommend the following best practices during the search.

Investigators should—

+ Repeat the neighborhood canvass the following day for the same timeframe of the abduction, starting 30 minutes before the time of the abduction. The Case Management for Missing Children Homicide Investigation study (see chapter 1, Overview of Existing Research) revealed that the murderer was in the area of initial contact two-thirds of the time because he or she lived in the area, was engaged in normal social activity, or worked in the area or was there on other business.

+ Look at the area from different views; e.g., obtain pictures taken from a helicopter and study satellite images, if possible. Researchers found that the victim's last known location was usually very close to the site of the initial contact between the killer and the victim. When police did not know the initial contact site, the solution rate dropped to 24 percent from 80 percent when police knew the initial contact site.

+ During the investigation, give special attention to individuals who recently moved into or away from the area. The Case Management for Missing Children Homicide Investigation study revealed that after the crime was committed, 16 percent of murderers left town and 10 percent interjected themselves into the murder investigation.

+ Check all registered sex offenders in the area and verify this information against any database that contains information about these individuals. If the local agency cannot generate a list of all offenders who work or live within the radius of the abduction, investigators should check with the state sex offender registry to see if that system can perform such a search.

Practitioner Tip: Electronic Surveillance

With the advent of smart phones, GPS systems, and other wireless devices, agencies should consider contacting local, state, or federal subject-matter experts who may have the equipment and ability to locate persons via specialized tracking technology. If this resource is not available within the agency's jurisdiction, the agency should contact the nearest U.S. Marshal's office for assistance.

Use of Volunteers During the Search

Volunteers can be an asset in the search and recovery of a missing child; however, if not properly screened, trained, and prepared, they can compromise the operation. An agency-assigned volunteer coordinator should create a plan that specifies how volunteers will be used as a resource in missing child cases.

Types of Volunteers

Agencies can incorporate a volunteer protocol within their plan in one of two ways. They can use a predetermined corps of volunteers who are selected and trained for use in child abductions or other incidents, or they can specify procedures to be used when an incident occurs and volunteers are needed or asked to assist. Both established volunteer groups and individual volunteers offer skills and resources that can be used before, during, and after an emergency.

Some agencies have identified groups with whom they have a trusted relationship and who are approved to assist the agency in missing child investigations and other local emergencies. Such groups include local search and rescue teams, citizen police academy graduates, and auxiliary officers. Some agencies have a volunteer program and actively solicit volunteers to be used in various components within their agency.

If an agency does not have a predetermined corps of volunteers, then the agency protocol should include procedures to address spontaneous volunteers who show up onsite to offer their services. Due to lack of training and orientation, spontaneous volunteers can create extra work for responders who are forced to direct volunteers rather than focus on their primary job, thereby interfering with the response. The agency must have a plan to channel this valuable resource appropriately and effectively.

Resource: Pools of Trained Volunteers

Examples of trained volunteers include:

+ National Center for Missing & Exploited Children (www.missingkids.com)

  • Project ALERT (America's Law Enforcement Retiree Team).

  • Team HOPE.

  • Team Adam.

+ Emergency response teams.

+ Search and rescue teams.

+ Explorers, recruits, and military reserve units.

+ Citizen police academy participants and alumni.

+ National Guard units.

The U.S. military is authorized to assist local jurisdictions in the event of a missing child. Contact the Air Force Rescue Coordination Center Console Operations at 850–283–5955/5347/5348/5349.

Managing Volunteers

Once volunteers have been identified, the volunteer coordinator should do the following:

+ Conduct background checks on volunteers or use volunteers who have already been cleared by background checks.

+ Obtain a photograph and/or videotape of all volunteers.

+ Distribute identification badges (with pictures) to the volunteers.

+ Ensure volunteers have correctly completed registration and waiver of liability forms. (Sample forms can be obtained by contacting the AMBER Alert Training and Technical Assistance program at AskAMBER@fvtc.edu.)

+ Maintain a log of each volunteer's name, date of birth, phone numbers, and address, and update it quarterly. If applicable, include an inventory of their skills and expertise.

+ Hold periodic training sessions with identified volunteers. Suggested topics include:

  • Issues surrounding missing and abducted children.

  • Protocols to be followed during the search.

  • Roleplays of the protocols as practice exercises.

  • Review of laws regarding locations in which volunteers are legally allowed to search.

  • Safety issues.

  • The importance of staying with an assigned "buddy" or other team members.

  • What to do if a volunteer witnesses an incident or finds potential evidence.

If volunteers are used in the search efforts, the coordinator should:

+ Instruct volunteers not to talk to the media—all announcements and updates will come only from the designated media representative.

+ Remind volunteers that they cannot discuss case-related activities with family or friends.

+ Maintain control over the search, volunteers, public safety personnel, and others.

+ Check with volunteers periodically for signs of stress or fatigue.

+ Rotate volunteers because some may become tired or need to leave.

+ Make sure food and drinks are provided for volunteers during the search.

+ Ensure that volunteers are closely supervised and consider assigning a law enforcement officer to each search group.

When the search has concluded, the coordinator should:

+ Remind volunteers about the confidential nature of information about the case.

+ Give volunteers as much information about the case as the investigation will allow.

+ Make sure that volunteers know why some information about the case cannot be disclosed.

+ Thank volunteers for helping with the search.

+ If possible, write thank-you notes to the volunteers within 2 weeks.

Taking care of volunteers and expressing appreciation is the best way to ensure participation in future searches.

Practitioner Tip: Debriefing

Although every law enforcement agency should establish and regularly update its policies and procedures, the local agency should conduct a debriefing after issuing an alert to evaluate the effectiveness of the total incident response and make recommendations, if needed, for improving its AMBER Alert plan.

The Family Perspective

At least once a year, the Office of Justice Programs convenes a roundtable composed of family members and survivors of missing and/or abducted children. The participants have endured the horror associated with the abduction and, in most cases, the murder or the nonrecovery of their child. Although it is difficult for family members to participate in the roundtable, many do so to share their experience and to help law enforcement and other partners understand how having a missing or abducted child affects a family. In addition, family members offer invaluable information on what law enforcement did well and what they could have done better during the investigation.

Following is some of the feedback received from family members in regard to law enforcement's initial response:

+ Officers should act immediately and treat the case as an endangered missing child case.

+ Officers should ask the parents for a recent photo of the missing child.

+ Officers should treat the home as a crime scene but attempt to leave the home in the condition in which they found it.

+ Officers should give parents the details, even the hard ones, before they give information to the media.

+ Officers should never assume the child is a runaway or make statements such as "They will probably come home in a few days." If the missing child is a teenager, law enforcement can be quick to stereotype him or her as a runaway; this assumption can hinder the immediate implementation of a plan to find the missing child. It is important for law enforcement to trust what the parents are saying and verify the information.

+ Law enforcement needs to understand compliant behavior and the dynamics of abduction-seduction, also known as "learned helplessness," so as not to make assumptions or draw incorrect conclusions when investigating cases where a child willingly left or stayed with the abductor even if the child may have had opportunities to escape.

+ The family's socioeconomic status should not make a difference in how law enforcement handles a case.

+ Every first responder should use a checklist when investigating a case to ensure that certain strategies are not accidently omitted during the chaos often associated with these types of events.

+ Inservice training on the policies and procedures of missing children cases should be mandated for officers, and officers should be recertified at least once every 2 years.

+ Crime scene professionals should be trained on the importance of evidence collection and preservation in missing children cases.

+ Law enforcement agencies should have the capability to rapidly deploy tracking dogs in high-risk missing children cases.

+ Law enforcement could benefit from training on how to question parents in a way that allows them to gather information while being sensitive to what the parents are going through.

Resources: Family Resource Guides

The Office of Juvenile Justice and Delinquency Prevention has published *When Your Child Is Missing: A Family Survival Guide, What About Me? Coping With the Abduction of a Brother or Sister,* and *The Crime of Family Abduction: A Child's and Parent's Perspective.* The publications are available in English and Spanish at www.ojjdp.gov/childabduction.html. Victim advocates should locate and share these resources with family members.

Chapter 4. Partnership With the Media

The media can be a vital ally in the search for a missing child. Broadcasters who enter into agreements with law enforcement agencies to provide immediate response during AMBER Alerts should be assured that their partner agencies will fulfill all of their responsibilities in accordance with the activation plan. Some of these responsibilities may be detailed in a memorandum of understanding (MOU).

To maintain confidence in the AMBER Alert system, all partners should agree to the following:

+ To protect the integrity of the AMBER Alert system and prevent transmission of false or misleading information to the media, the system will include special codes and privileged activation transmissions for plan partners and stakeholders.

+ Law enforcement officials will request broadcast time to alert the public only when all previously established criteria have been met.

+ Law enforcement officials will provide complete, thorough information that is not legally prohibited and does not jeopardize the integrity of an investigation or the child's safe rescue.

+ Law enforcement officials will recognize that broadcasters have a responsibility to the public to provide accurate information; therefore, law enforcement should confirm speculative reports.

+ Law enforcement officials will quickly terminate an AMBER Alert when the threat is no longer imminent or apparent or when the child is rescued, even if the suspect is still at large. AMBER Alerts are for the child, not the suspect.

+ The AMBER Alert will include a phone number for the public to call.

+ Law enforcement officials and other authorities, such as 911 centers, will provide a method for handling the tips and inquiries called into the phone number once the AMBER Alert has been activated.

+ Activation of an AMBER Alert will not prevent news organizations, including stations airing AMBER Alerts, from using this information for legitimate news purposes.

+ Information gleaned by legitimate news operations but not provided in the AMBER Alert announcement can be disseminated to the public in news broadcasts and newspapers.

+ Law enforcement will establish procedures for making information available, when possible, to the media and to other law enforcement agencies before requesting an alert.

+ Law enforcement and the media will agree to provide the equipment, time, and personnel necessary for periodic tests of the system used for alerting the media. These tests will be conducted by the Emergency Alert System and the National Oceanic and Atmospheric Administration and will be disseminated by fax, e-mail, and other means.

+ The official, approved AMBER Alert cannot be altered without the permission of the issuing law enforcement agency.

Verification of Information

AMBER Alert situations are fluid and change minute by minute. Therefore, during an alert, law enforcement officials should be accessible to their media partners, and the agency should provide a way for reporters to verify information gathered during normal newsroom operations.

An up-to-date Web site can be extremely useful for this purpose. In addition, an agency point of contact for the media should be appointed and all updated information should come from that liaison.

Message Content

AMBER Alerts must be concise, immediately understood, easily assimilated, and quickly disseminated, and should not contain any abbreviations or police jargon. Except under extraordinary circumstances, an AMBER Alert should be no longer than one to four sentences and should use the fewest words possible without compromising clarity. It is critical to include specific descriptors that would make the child and/or suspect stand out from the rest of the population.

The alert message should be derived from the following information:

+ Specific information about the incident, including day, time, location, and other details.

+ Name, age, and gender of the abducted child along with physical descriptive information (e.g., height, weight, birthmarks, hair color, eye color, and clothing).

+ Confirmation (if applicable) that the suspect is listed in the state sex offender registry.

+ A description of the suspect's vehicle, including license plate number and state of issuance, and a photo of the vehicle model, if available.

+ Roads and highways believed to be used by the suspect, if known.

+ Other methods of transportation (such as taxi, bus, train, or airplane) that the suspect may use.

+ Town, community, or state where the suspect and abducted child may be traveling.

+ Confirmation that law enforcement believes the child is in imminent danger.

+ Reasons why law enforcement believes the child is in danger and why law enforcement believes the suspect is traveling to a certain destination or via a certain route.

+ Toll-free telephone numbers for the public to call authorities if they observe the suspect or abducted child.

Additional details about the missing child that are available to the public but not included in the alert should be provided to the news media and can be part of the initial press release. The content of the AMBER Alert will directly affect the effectiveness of the alert; therefore, it is critical that broadcasters maintain the wording that the law enforcement agency provides.

Sample Emergency Alert Message

The Metropolitan Police Department is searching for 10-year-old Jane Doe. She was abducted around 4 p.m. while walking near the corner of Nebraska Avenue and Reno Road in northwest Washington. Jane is approximately 4 feet tall, weighs about 60 pounds, has short brown hair and brown eyes, and is Caucasian. She was wearing a blue T-shirt, blue jeans, and a red hat. The suspect is a white man in his 20s, approximately 5 feet 10 inches tall, 200 pounds, and has short black hair. He was driving a bright red Ford Bronco that was last seen heading north on Connecticut Avenue toward I-495. If you have any information regarding this abduction, call the Metropolitan Police Department immediately at 202–XXX–XXXX.

Additional information about how to broadcast AMBER Alerts appropriately can be found in the National Center for Missing & Exploited Children publication, *AMBER Alert: Law Enforcement and Broadcaster Guide* (www.ncmec.org/en_US/documents/AmberGuide.pdf).

Practitioner Tips: Broadcasting an Alert

Following are some guidelines concerning frequency and content when broadcasting AMBER Alerts:

+ Primary broadcast stations should consider reissuing an alert every 30 minutes or more often, as appropriate, in prime viewing and listening periods. Consideration may be given to the first natural break within the 30-minute time period.

+ Messages that contain updated information from law enforcement should be broadcast as necessary until the law enforcement agency terminates the alert.

+ A televised message should include an audio alert announcement and an onscreen visual announcement or a message that "crawls" across the bottom of the screen.

+ A televised message should include a phone number for the public to call. The phone number should be repeated at least twice during each announcement.

+ A radio message should include specific details and a phone number for the public to call. The phone number should be repeated at least twice during each announcement.

+ The number of times an AMBER Alert is announced should not be reduced prior to deactivation of the alert by law enforcement unless appropriate law enforcement officials have been notified (these issues should be resolved in a memorandum of understanding or in other guidelines).

+ Plans should be made for "unmanned" stations if there is an automatic termination after a certain period of time. If the child is found prior to the defined period of time, then an Emergency Alert System cancellation message can turn off the unmanned stations.

Sensitivity to the Audience

Targeting key audiences is an important aspect of an AMBER Alert. The goal is to notify the people who will most likely be in a position to use the information to aid in the child's recovery. AMBER Alerts must be carefully constructed to avoid further victimization of the child or the use of any word or phrase that could alienate someone who might otherwise be willing to help in the search. Particular care should be given to any mention of the following:

+ Physical or mental disabilities (unless pertinent to a physical description).

+ Identifying the victimization of the child to the public.

+ Sexual preference of the abductor (except where applicable, such as being listed in a state sex offender registry).

+ Political affiliation.

+ Religious preference.

+ Other sensitive information that has no bearing on locating an abducted child.

Message Frequency

The frequency of announcements is a critical component of the AMBER Alert plan. Broadcast media representatives sometimes wrestle with the issue of how frequently an AMBER Alert should be transmitted. AMBER Alert Coordinators should work closely with broadcasters (primary, cable, and secondary) in their area to establish a clear plan of operation for how quickly and how often the primary alerting station will issue an AMBER Alert. These decisions should be delineated in formal MOUs or other agreements before implementing the AMBER Alert plan.

Other Considerations

The broadcast media voluntarily provide their valuable airtime to inform the public that a child has been abducted in the belief that such information is in the best interest of the community. In exchange for this assistance, broadcasters can reasonably expect the following:

+ An alert was issued based on previously agreed-upon criteria.

+ Broadcasters will have access to law enforcement to the extent possible, understanding the investigation must take precedence.

+ An alert will be terminated as soon as it has been determined that the announcement is no longer needed.

It is critical that the lines of communication between broadcasters and law enforcement officials be kept open at all times. The safe return of the abducted child must remain the paramount concern and focus.

Chapter 5. The Role of a Public Information Officer

Keeping the child's image in the mind of the public is key to the investigation. The intense media coverage during an AMBER Alert has directly led to the recovery of the child and in some cases has even resulted in the abductor releasing the child in an effort to avoid apprehension. The Public Information Officer's (PIO's) primary function during an AMBER Alert is to convey accurate and timely information from the law enforcement agency to the public via the media and to keep the child's image and the story in the news.

A law enforcement agency's PIO performs the following essential functions in the AMBER Alert Program:

+ Notifies the public (via the media) to be on the lookout for a missing child.

+ Enhances media coverage of the missing child incident by providing photographs, videos, and other visual aids to help identify the victim(s) and/or suspect(s) and the vehicle(s) used in the abduction.

+ Ensures that the story stays alive by providing regular updates with accurate and timely information.

+ Gauges public opinions and media perceptions for the agency, addressing any issues and ensuring the focus stays on the child.

+ Anticipates possible worst-case scenarios and prepares the agency's response to the types of questions likely to accompany such scenarios.

+ Provides family members and friends with effective strategies for conducting media interviews and press conferences, safeguards investigatory details of the case, and, to the extent possible, protects the family's privacy.

+ Safeguards the continued partnership between the media and law enforcement.

The law enforcement agency's chief executive officer (CEO) must have confidence in the PIO and the PIO must be able to function within the CEO's authority. A CEO once commented that "activating an AMBER Alert is like sending up a flare asking every media outlet to critique the way you are handling your investigation." Although part of the PIO's job is to respond to questions about investigative efforts, the PIO must maintain the focus on the primary goal, which is to rescue and recover the missing child.

Ideally, the PIO should be involved in an AMBER Alert activation from the very beginning. It is time consuming for the PIO to try to catch up on the events leading up to an AMBER Alert or during an AMBER Alert. The best way to ensure the PIO is included in all aspects of the AMBER Alert process is to define the PIO's responsibilities clearly in the law enforcement agency's policies and procedures.

The procedures for AMBER Alerts should clearly identify steps for the PIO to follow, for example:

+ When and how to notify the media that an AMBER Alert has been issued.

+ How to handle or where to direct inquiries from the media.

+ How to handle or where to direct inquiries from the public.

The PIO's specific functions during an AMBER Alert activation may vary among agencies, but are likely to be similar in the following key ways:

+ The PIO either assists in or is immediately made aware of the decision to activate or deactivate an AMBER Alert.

+ The PIO is considered an essential member of the agency's incident management structure before, during, and after an AMBER Alert so that he or she understands all aspects of the operation.

Choosing a Public Information Officer

Law enforcement agencies vary in size, structure, and composition. Ideally, the PIO should work full time for the law enforcement agency and know how to release information to the public through the media. Larger agencies usually have a PIO in place to keep the public informed. Smaller agencies, on the other hand, often lack the personnel or resources to hire a dedicated PIO and may rely on other agencies within their jurisdiction or the state police to provide this service. Alternatively, a small agency without a full-time PIO could designate a key officer in advance to function as a PIO in the event of an alert. The designated officer should then be trained so that he or she can be effective in dealing with both the media and the public during an activation.

The PIO must be answerable to the chief or sheriff and must fully understand the intricate process of releasing information to the public. In addition, the PIO must have access to information, key agency personnel (including the chief or sheriff), the crime scene area, and other areas where information may be generated.

Once a primary PIO has been appointed, it may be useful to identify a backup PIO to assist or fill in if the primary PIO is absent. During an AMBER Alert incident, the PIO should only be responsible for disseminating information to the public that will help in the recovery of the abducted child, and if the normally designated PIO is also involved in the investigation then a backup PIO should be designated. This will allow key investigative personnel to focus exclusively on recovering the missing child safely and investigating the circumstances of the disappearance.

The PIO may wish to designate points of contact for specific information, but only the PIO should make this decision. In any case, the primary designated point of contact—the PIO—should remain the same.

Placement of the Public Information Officer Within the Incident Management System

The Incident Management System (IMS) represents National Incident Management System protocol as required by U.S. Department of Homeland Security statutory regulations. The PIO should be strategically placed within the IMS so that he or she has direct access to all law enforcement personnel in command of the operation. Access to information is essential for the PIO to establish a smooth flow of information to the public and monitor how well the media are disseminating details about the alert.

Figure 2 shows the optimal position of the PIO within the IMS, reporting directly to the incident commander but above and outside the command officer structure. This management structure gives the PIO access to the IMS commander and to the individual command officers who work with all of the investigative aspects of the AMBER Alert.

A PIO who is involved in the agency's key decisionmaking processes will be able to ensure that the media receive only responsible messages that will effectively inform the public about the agency's search for a missing child.

Duties of a Public Information Officer

AMBER Alert programs nationwide may differ in the policies that designate who is responsible for requesting activation or deactivation of an alert and the criteria that dictate when an alert is to be

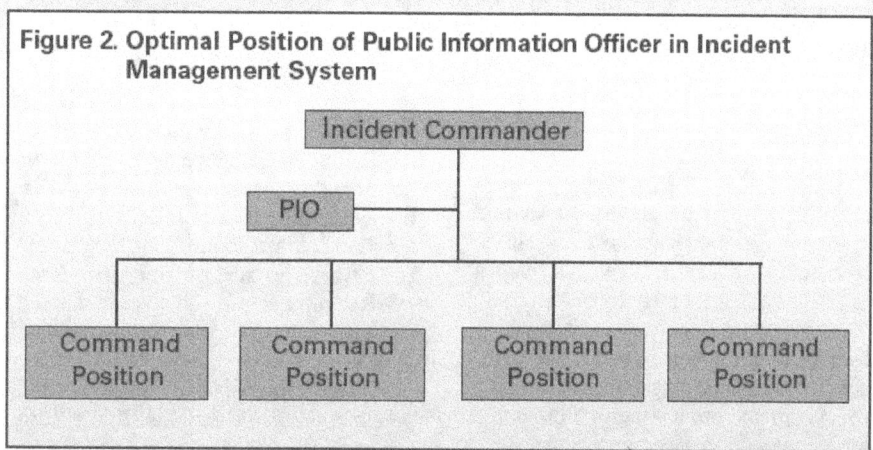

Figure 2. Optimal Position of Public Information Officer in Incident Management System

Incident Commander

PIO

Command Position

Command Position

Command Position

Command Position

activated or deactivated. In all cases, however, the PIO's role is to set the overall tone during an alert and to control the flow of information based on legal restrictions and agency policies.

No law enforcement agency should be without a PIO during this critical time of need for public and media assistance. The PIO's presence will be particularly prominent during the early stages of an AMBER Alert when press conferences, media interviews, and similar events will keep the PIO's name and face, but more importantly the child, in the public eye.

Organizing Media Briefings

The PIO should be responsible for all logistics involving media briefings, including creating the briefing schedule, establishing the location of the briefings (away from the command center if possible), and securing parking for media vehicles.

When conducting media briefings, the PIO should:

✦ Choose a location for the briefing area that will meet the needs of both investigators and the media. Consider parking lots and other public areas rather than law enforcement headquarters.

✦ Set the tone for the media briefing. Maintain control of the entire briefing environment (e.g., where it takes place, participants' roles, and structure of the briefing).

✦ Start every media briefing with an opening statement by an appropriate law enforcement official followed by a question-and-answer dialog (if previously agreed to by law enforcement officials).

✦ Provide additional information about the victim(s) and/or suspect(s) along with photographs and a home video (if available), as approved by command officials, to enhance the media's coverage of the incident.

✦ Enlist the aid of media technical personnel if copies of videotapes or audiotapes and live feeds are necessary (if family members and/or the commander in charge of the investigation have granted approval for their use).

✦ Disseminate photographs of selected crime scene areas as appropriate and with command officials' approval.

✦ Plan for a worst-case scenario by anticipating all types of questions that are likely to arise in such a scenario and the agency's response.

◆ Work with family members to prepare them if they are to be a part of the briefing.

Ensuring the Message Is Received

During the public warning phase, AMBER Alerts are usually disseminated through text messaging, which means the request for activation and public warning messages are most often in written form. Written messages are also found on U.S. Department of Transportation variable message signs and in television broadcasts, where a written text message "crawling" across the top or bottom of the television screen often accompanies or follows a verbal alert. A law enforcement agency generates all messages.

A PIO whose responsibilities include asking the media to broadcast an AMBER Alert also ensures that the request to disseminate the message has been understood and properly carried out. A PIO who does not have this responsibility should nevertheless verify, on behalf of his or her agency, that the request has been made.

The PIO should not assume an AMBER Alert has been received solely because it was sent by traditional means such as facsimile or e-mail. The PIO should do the following to verify that the media have received the AMBER Alert:

◆ Telephone the appropriate broadcast media representative for confirmation.

◆ Follow up with an e-mail or text message, where available.

Finally, the PIO should be prepared. An AMBER Alert can generate an immediate demand for information from all types of media, both local and national, and rapid updates of accurate information are critical. This sudden demand can be overwhelming, especially for a small agency.

Controlling the Spread of Rumors

Rumors and false or misleading information frequently emerge during any law enforcement incident or investigation, and AMBER Alerts are no exception. Because journalists will seek additional information on their own from a victim's family members, friends, and witnesses, rumors can develop quickly. It is important for the PIO to monitor rumors and stay informed about all aspects of the investigation. Fortunately, the PIO is in a strategic position to control the information delivered to the public and thus help eliminate potential problems early on. The PIO should do the following:

◆ Monitor all media coverage of an AMBER Alert incident, including special alert announcements, continuing news media coverage, television and radio talk shows, and Web sites that conventional and nonconventional media maintain.

◆ Collect as much information as possible about any circulating rumors and be vigilant in refuting any incorrect or misleading reports.

◆ Contact the appropriate news media outlet to address incorrect information directly or issue a special agencywide news announcement that specifies the correct information to be conveyed to the public.

◆ Recognize that the media are participating voluntarily in an AMBER Alert and do not wish to be viewed as an extension of law enforcement. The media respect law enforcement agencies much more when those agencies recognize that the media's primary responsibility is to inform the public independently.

◆ Be aware that once an AMBER Alert has been activated, the story will be pursued aggressively. This means the "angle" of the story may change in unpredictable ways. For example, the AMBER Alert process may be analyzed, the criminal investigation may be scrutinized, and the public's response may be evaluated—all in the public domain—with little or no direction from law enforcement.

+ Make no attempt to seize media videotapes or audiotapes (whether broadcast or out-takes), notes, photographs, or other material that is owned by or in the possession of the media. Frequently, the media will honor a request for a copy of the material.

Finally, as a representative of law enforcement, the PIO should be aware that some information that the media uncovers may need to be investigated.

The PIO's Role in the Deactivation Phase

The AMBER Alert should be deactivated when the child is recovered even if the suspect is still at large. The deactivation of an AMBER Alert will likely lead to additional responsibilities for the PIO. The PIO should do the following:

+ Inform victims' families about the most effective ways to deal with media attention and the pros and cons of being interviewed by the media. In addition, the PIO should let the families know about information they should and should not discuss, in accordance with the advice of investigators and prosecutors working on the case. (See the "Resources: Family Resource Guides" sidebar in chapter 3.)

+ Work with the prosecuting attorney to ensure that the release of information will not

jeopardize the ability to obtain a conviction in the case if the subject was arrested or in the event the subject is later located and charged.

+ Acknowledge on behalf of the agency and its CEO the contributions of everyone involved, including broadcasters, local businesses, volunteers, government agencies, and law enforcement agencies that supported the effort with additional manpower and other resources. The CEO may wish to handle this task personally; however, whoever conducts this briefing should do the following:

  • Acknowledge and thank all media representatives, including newspapers, cell phone providers, and co-owned Web-based services, for their assistance in publicizing the AMBER Alert.

  • Acknowledge and thank other organizations and volunteers that donated time and services on behalf of the missing child (e.g., utility companies, taxicab companies, various nonprofit organizations, and other groups and businesses).

  • Acknowledge and thank all law enforcement agencies (federal, state, and local) that participated in both the search and investigative phases of the incident.

Ultimately, the PIO's role in an AMBER Alert is fluid. His or her functions can change with each new set of circumstances. Above all, the PIO must remember that once an AMBER Alert has been issued, it is public information and cannot be taken back. Also, the alert does not end until proper deactivation procedures have been completed.

Chapter 6. Effective Messaging Strategies

Almost 90 percent of AMBER Alert plans use the Emergency Alert System (EAS) to disseminate an alert. The remaining plans use the National Weather Service or a system of their own design, such as facsimile or e-mail transmissions from law enforcement agencies to individual media outlets. In 2004, the U.S. Department of Transportation published *AMBER, Emergency, and Travel Time Messaging Guidance for Transportation Agencies.* The information that follows is adapted from the report. The full report is available at www.ops.fhwa.dot.gov/TravelInfo/resources/cms_rept/cmspractices.pdf.

Process and Operations

Initiation of an AMBER Alert is always the responsibility of an emergency management or law enforcement agency, such as state or local police or the office of emergency management. Information to post, update, and remove alerts is often sent via fax to the state's department of transportation (DOT) or via local methods for using the EAS.

Some jurisdictions have a programmed list of preplanned scenarios (i.e., templates into which an operator will insert the details relevant to the particular situation); other DOTs receive instruction on how to structure the message.

Message Content

The text displayed on variable message signs (VMS) during an AMBER Alert varies significantly. The text varies from state to state, and many states are revising their policies and now display messages differently from one alert to the next. The amount of information available to law enforcement (and by extension to the DOT) can also vary, which makes standardization a challenge. For example, transportation management center operators at one state DOT had minimal information and posted the following message:

"AMBER ALERT

CALL 911"

This was widely seen as a failure because no specific information (such as vehicle description or tag number) was given to help locate the vehicle involved, and many motorists were not yet familiar with AMBER Alerts at that time. The jurisdiction's 911 dispatch center was inundated with calls from confused motorists.

Although a vehicle description is generally part of the text displayed during an AMBER Alert, there is disagreement regarding whether or not to post the entire vehicle license plate number. Some jurisdictions consider that a license plate number is too much information for a motorist to absorb while driving at freeway speeds, and instead prefer to advise motorists to tune to local news radio stations to obtain more information. Others think that posting a vehicle description without a license plate number may contribute to vigilante behavior on the part of a motorist who sees a vehicle that matches the description. However, it should be noted that children have been successfully recovered as a result of someone recalling the description and vehicle tag information.

Many jurisdictions use a similar order of information in AMBER Alerts. Most jurisdictions generally use three lines to convey an AMBER Alert, and the order tends to be: general category of information on the first line, vehicle information on the second line, and desired motorist response on the third line. Two pages are usually used to convey all information pertinent to the alert.

Examples of wording include the following:

(Page 1)

"CHILD ABDUCTION"

"RED FORD"

"CALL 911"

(Page 2)

"CHILD ABDUCTION"

"LIC # ABC 123"

"CALL 911"

One state indicated that it does not use the term "AMBER Alert" on its VMS because of a concern that motorists will confuse the text with a change in the national security threat level. Instead, this state posts "CHILD ABDUCTION" on the first line of the VMS during an AMBER Alert activation.

Message Readability

In some states, guidelines regarding sign readability call for a minimum of 900 feet of visibility, which translates to 8.8 seconds of viewing time at 70 mph or 11 seconds at 55 mph. A rule of thumb in practice when using VMS is that the minimum exposure time should be at least 2 seconds per line. Arizona State University studied the legibility of various VMS in the Phoenix area and concluded that fiber optic VMS have an average legibility of approximately 835 feet. Subtracting 150 feet because of vehicle cutoff (i.e., the sign is hidden from the driver because it is obscured by the vehicle's roof as the vehicle approaches the VMS) leaves an average reading distance of 685 feet. Thus, motorists have approximately 6 seconds to comprehend a VMS message at 75 mph or 7 seconds at 65 mph.

In the states that were studied, signs consisted of 2 to 3 lines per page, 16 to 28 characters per line, and 10 to 18 inches per character. Most signs are capable of displaying two pages and some signs can display four consecutive pages; however, many states insist that it is not safe to display more than one page to drivers traveling at freeway speeds. Some signs are capable of providing more elaborate presentations: different fonts, flashing, centering, or justifying text right or left.

Message Construction

Message construction refers to standard words, phrases, and abbreviations. There is little variability in message construction. Word and phrase libraries tend to be relatively similar; the major differences occur in the formality of the message structure.

Message construction in some DOTs follows a specific outline, for example:

✦ State the problem being addressed.

✦ Describe the location.

✦ Define what the motorist is being asked to do.

It is important to achieve a balance between the impacts of these three elements. If one of them is overemphasized, the result is that others may be neglected or messages may become too long or complex. In addition, consistency in style and order allows the motorist to anticipate the message and to focus on the element line that he or she deems most important. When more than one page is available, messages are still often constructed to fit on one page to maximize readability.

Policies and Practices

Policies regarding the posting, updating, and removal of AMBER Alerts are generally not the domain of DOTs. The DOT's role in disseminating AMBER Alerts is widely accepted as supplementary; they receive the information, inform the public via VMS, and instruct motorists to respond accordingly (e.g., call 911 or another abbreviated phone number, or tune to local media for detailed information). Some DOTs, however, desire a more active role in determining the template for the message and the length of time the message is posted. They may have liability concerns, and they may want a hierarchical plan to handle alerts that are requested when a dangerous driving condition is also being posted. Transportation staff have experience with motorists, and their thoughts and ideas should be carefully considered.

The amount of time an AMBER Alert remains active varies greatly. Some DOTs keep an AMBER Alert on VMS for a set amount of time (usually between 3 and 8 hours). One state's DOT specifies in its policy that alerts must be kept on VMS for 8 hours from the time of initiation, and that the time may be extended whenever there is an update to the alert. Another state has a policy that stipulates the removal of an alert after 1 hour if it occurs during rush hour and after 4 hours during nonpeak periods. Other state DOTs wait for the managing law enforcement agency to advise the DOT to deactivate the alert.

Permanent Versus Portable Variable Message Signs

Message construction varies for permanent and portable VMS. Portable signs are generally smaller and able to handle fewer characters per line than permanent signs. Portable signs can accommodate two lines of text, and permanent signs can accommodate three lines. For example, the Arizona Department of Transportation's permanent signs use 3 lines with 18 characters per line, and its portable signs use 3 lines with 10 characters per line. Messages are displayed on two pages whenever possible.

Although AMBER Alerts are generally posted either on all permanent VMS or on those within a specified radius, posting of AMBER Alerts on portable VMS tends to be at the discretion of the transportation management center supervisor on duty.

Frequency of Use

The frequency of using VMS is a significant and widely discussed issue, and contradictory attitudes exist on this subject. Transportation officials consider that VMS should be used rarely and thereby retain the ability to attract a motorist's attention (i.e., text on a VMS indicates that unusual conditions are occurring). On the other hand, feedback from many DOTs suggests that the traveling public does not like to see the signs remain blank

because it gives the impression that the signs are nothing more than a rarely used expensive toy.

Results

The overall response to the use of messaging signs during AMBER Alerts is consistently positive nationwide. In general, the public views the use of VMS for AMBER Alerts as a valuable use

Success Story: Variable Message Signs

In 2009, an AMBER Alert was issued for a young child in Sanford, NH. Michael Grant heard the alert on the radio and saw the variable message signs while driving home from work. Later that day, Grant saw the vehicle and, thanks to the AMBER Alert and his attentiveness, the child was rescued and returned to her mother.

"My wife and I and the kids were all sitting down to have supper and the AMBER Alert had come on the news and it was broadcast that a man had taken off with a 2-year-old girl ... . We got a lot of construction going on in New Hampshire right now. So, you know the digital signs they use to tell you to slow down because there is somebody in the road? They converted all the signs over and they all said 1999 Dodge green pickup truck with the Maine license plate number ... .And I thought that was incredible to ... utilize the signs that belong to construction companies ... . I saw them [the signs] all the way home. You couldn't miss them and I think that's kind of what instilled into me to memorize a lot of stuff.

"I had gone hunting that day and as I started heading down a dirt road, I saw the truck and then I saw the plate ... put two and two together, realized it was the green truck ... as I was just standing there, I finally saw the little girl jump up on the seat ... . I thought, I'm committed to this now, because I saw the little girl. I got two kids of my own and I realized then that it's my job to make sure that child's brought home."

—Michael M. Grant, Jr.
Recipient of U.S. Department of Justice's
2010 AMBER Alert Citizen Award

of the equipment. Some states have experienced positive results with AMBER Alert messages; for example, California saw a high-visibility success with the safe return of two teenage girls who had been abducted by a stranger. Many states claim that since implementing their AMBER Alert plans, every alert has resulted in the safe return of the abducted child.

Chapter 7. The Role of the AMBER Alert Coordinator

A critical stakeholder group in an AMBER Alert plan includes the national, state, local, and regional AMBER Alert Coordinators. The Assistant Attorney General for the Office of Justice Programs is the National AMBER Alert Coordinator, whose role is to help state and local officials develop and enhance AMBER Alert plans and promote statewide and regional coordination among plans.

The state or local AMBER Alert Coordinator oversees the implementation, maintenance, and enhancement of the AMBER Alert Program. The position is usually housed within a state or local law enforcement agency; however, a few states have chosen members of the broadcast community to fill this critical role. A list of state AMBER Alert Coordinators is available at www.amberalert.gov/state_contacts.htm.

Duties of the AMBER Alert Coordinator

The Coordinator's tasks may include:

+ Developing and maintaining AMBER Alert criteria and any procedures for activating and denying AMBER Alerts.

+ Overseeing the AMBER Alert activation process.

+ Overseeing the AMBER Alert activation review committee.

+ Coordinating with AMBER Alert partners and stakeholders.

+ Developing and maintaining the oversight committee.

+ Maintaining any guidelines, procedures, or memoranda of understanding.

+ Coordinating AMBER Alert training for law enforcement, broadcasters, transportation officials, and any other identified partners.

+ Providing public awareness and marketing of the AMBER Alert Program.

+ Developing and distributing education materials.

+ Communicating with representatives from the AMBER Alert Program.

+ Communicating with other Coordinators via the AMBER Alert Portal.

+ Ensuring that secondary alerts are administered appropriately.

+ Overseeing any other endangered alert systems that are in place when an AMBER Alert cannot be used in a specific situation.

+ Ensuring that "Child Abduction" and "AMBER Alert" flags are entered appropriately in the National Crime Information Center.

The Coordinator's role varies from state to state; the responsibilities could include approval of activations, conducting after-action debriefings, marketing the program, and training. Some of the Coordinator's responsibilities, along with practitioner tips for carrying out these duties effectively, are presented below.

Administration

The AMBER Alert Coordinator is responsible for ensuring that the program is institutionalized within the jurisdiction and that all partners are engaged and are maintaining the agreed-upon components. The Coordinator's administrative functions include development and maintenance of AMBER materials and procedures.

Practitioners recommend that the AMBER Alert Coordinator—

✦ Institute a process to review and update all procedures and materials annually.

✦ Consider adding redundancy in the Coordinator position to ensure consistency in case the Coordinator is transferred or to prepare for succession planning.

✦ Perform periodic tests of the system to ensure that the process will work when needed.

Maintaining Memorandums of Understanding

AMBER Alert Coordinators are encouraged to develop procedures and guidelines to ensure that criteria are adhered to and activations are timely. These procedures should be codified in a memorandum of understanding (MOU) with the various partner agencies. MOUs (or operating agreements) are living documents that have demonstrated their importance in the AMBER Alert Program. They help ensure that all stakeholders and partners are aware of and agree to the processes and procedures used to issue an AMBER Alert. They specify each stakeholder's duties and responsibilities and explain how communities and

jurisdictions will work together to protect the lives of children. Effective MOUs also include a general discussion of child recovery plans and strategies and how the AMBER Alert plan fits into the broader context.

A sample MOU can be obtained by contacting the AMBER Alert Training and Technical Assistance Program at AskAMBER@fvtc.edu.

Securing Funding

The AMBER Alert process leverages existing resources within a jurisdiction, and therefore it is a cost-effective tool in the investigation of a missing child. However, costs to maintain the program and provide training and awareness can deplete an agency's budget. Several programs have established foundations to supplement their budgets through fundraisers, donations, and gifts.

Several state AMBER Alert programs have mechanisms to collect donations. The Chamber of Commerce in Utah has sponsored conferences and provided financial support to the program. Minnesota has also accepted donations supplied to them through a partnership with the Jacob Wetterling Foundation. A regional program in Texas received funds through a golf tournament.

Coordinators can share ideas about funding through the AMBER Alert Portal and *The AMBER Advocate.*

Promoting Communication

Experienced AMBER Alert Coordinators strongly emphasize consistent and frequent communication with all partners; communication with the public through AMBER Alert Web sites; and maintaining contact with other Coordinators, the AMBER Alert Training and Technical Assistance Program, the National Center for Missing & Exploited Children (NCMEC), and the Department of Justice (DOJ) through the AMBER Alert Portal and *The AMBER Advocate* (see "Resource: The AMBER Alert Portal").

Resource: The AMBER Alert Portal

The AMBER Alert Portal on the Criminal Justice Collaboration Portal is an official interactive Web site for sharing information and support. It was created specifically for AMBER Alert Coordinators, Clearinghouse Managers, and Child Abduction Response Team Coordinators. The secure Web site informs AMBER Alert partners of the latest news, information, and resources. Discussion boards, shared document libraries, and other collaborative resources are available to facilitate effective work among AMBER Alert partners across the country and around the globe.

Also accessible via the portal are *The AMBER Advocate* (the official newsletter of the program with more than 40,000 recipients), recent success stories, announcements, and AMBER Alert partners. Additional links are provided for the AMBER Alert Program, the AMBER Alert Training and Technical Assistance Program, the Department of Justice Child Exploitation and Obscenity Section, and the National Center for Missing & Exploited Children. Also available on the portal are the AMBER Alert Legal Database and information about wireless AMBER Alerts.

For more information about the AMBER Alert Portal or to learn how Coordinators can gain access to the Criminal Justice Collaboration Portal, contact your regional AMBER Alert liaison or go to www.thecjportal.org/AmberAlert and click on "Contact us."

Scheduling and Overseeing Training

Coordinators should ensure that program participants receive necessary training and that new stakeholder agency staff receive training regularly. Training can be accomplished in a variety of ways that include formal scheduled sessions, Web-based or online training, distance learning, train-the-trainer sessions, and published materials.

Practitioners recommend that the AMBER Alert Coordinator—

+ Consider conducting joint training sessions that involve representatives from each partner group.

+ Use Webinars to provide training, which will eliminate travel expenses for both trainers and agencies.

+ Reinforce training and promote training opportunities by developing AMBER Alert pocket cards, breakroom posters, brochures, and other materials to enhance awareness of the program and to educate stakeholders on activation procedures.

+ Ensure that first responders receive necessary training and training materials and that they share this information with agency command staff.

+ Provide law enforcement agencies with sample policies they can use that can incorporate AMBER Alert into the agency's comprehensive response to a missing child.

+ Encourage states to incorporate AMBER Alert procedures into the state standards and training curriculum and to petition their legislature to mandate AMBER Alert training as part of the state's mandatory retraining curriculum.

+ Identify and distribute available training opportunities to AMBER Alert partners.

Resource: The AMBER Alert Training and Technical Assistance Program

The AMBER Alert Training and Technical Assistance Program has delivered training and technical assistance to more than 16,000 law enforcement personnel, prosecutors, child protection professionals, media representatives, and private-sector organizations. Visit www.amber-net.org/technicalassistance.html.

✦ Provide AMBER Alert training through professional organizations such as broadcasters', police chiefs', and sheriffs' associations.

Selecting the Right Technology To Promote the Alert

Access to the latest technical solutions can cut down on unnecessary delays once the call is made to activate an alert. This technology can automate notifications to the various partners and stakeholders, including the broadcast community and the emergency operations center, and send out any secondary alerts. Before purchasing technology or engaging in a partnership with a company to use technology, however, AMBER Alert Coordinators should check with other Coordinators, the National Center for Missing & Exploited Children, and DOJ to see if the technology is available without purchase or if any other Coordinators have had any experiences with the technology.

Circumstances surrounding an alert could mean that an activation must be expanded outside of a jurisdiction or state. Therefore, it is important to know the procedures for activating an alert in other states, and Coordinators should have all necessary contact information for AMBER Alert Coordinators in other states.

Selecting the proper technology for a community's needs can be a difficult and confusing task, and it is important to consider all options carefully. It is critical to select the best option based on research. Coordinators should consider consulting an information technology consultant, if one is available.

Consider the following questions when researching a technology solution or vendor and before purchasing the technology:

✦ What is the company's marketing plan?

- Does the company's income depend on the number of "hits" on its Web site? If so, the Coordinator must be vigilant of methods

that are more concerned with redirecting users to click on the Web site than with sending information quickly to those in the alert's geographical area.

- Does the technology send the AMBER Alerts outside the geographic area defined in the alert? For AMBER Alerts, quality and geographic targeting are the most important considerations, and a larger subscriber base could result in a slower system. In addition, individuals who receive alerts that do not apply to them may become desensitized and drop out of the program. Note: When demonstrating the technology's capabilities to a potential buyer, the vendor will most likely place the purchaser's e-mail address at the top of the list, ensuring speedy delivery. Individuals testing the system may want to consider using an alias e-mail address to test the system properly.

✦ Does the technology vendor use the agency's name to market its products?

- Coordinators may want to consider entering into an MOU that states the vendor cannot use the agency's name unless approval is received first.

- Remember, a technology vendor is *not* a partner.

✦ Does the technology vendor make false or misleading claims?

- As stated previously, research all aspects of the technology and the vendor.

- False information can frustrate participants and they may drop out of the program. In addition, false information damages the credibility of the AMBER Alert Program.

✦ Does the technology vendor ask for biographical data from those who are signing up? Anything more than an e-mail address can be used for marketing or can give the appearance that the information is being sold to marketers.

Testing the System

Scheduled testing of equipment and personnel should be conducted to maintain the optimal performance of the AMBER Alert system. The testing should involve every aspect of the system, including the technology that disseminates the alert information and the personnel who decide to activate the system. The testing process should employ various scenarios, including redundant backup plans in case of system failure.

Equipment testing should be done systematically; the AMBER Alert Coordinator should seek input or guidance from each primary stakeholder and partner to test the system consistently, effectively, and efficiently.

When using an outside system to assist the agency in its distribution of the AMBER Alert, it is important to ensure security measures are in place to protect personal identifying information within the system and to protect the system from any breaches that could result in the issuance of a false AMBER Alert to subscribers.

Practitioners recommend that the AMBER Alert Coordinator—

✦ Document training and practice the AMBER Alert notification procedure.

Resource: AMBER Alert Secondary Distribution

Recipients of AMBER Alert information can be divided into primary and secondary receivers. Primary receivers, such as the media and broadcasters, are responsible for disseminating the alert to a much larger audience. Secondary receivers include all of the remaining individuals who sign up to receive AMBER Alerts. Some Coordinators solicit the public to sign up to receive e-mail alerts. Although this is helpful, it is important to note that as more people sign up, the speed of dissemination decreases, depending on the specific network, and the primary receivers who are responsible for much larger disseminations will most likely experience delays. Therefore, it is advisable to maintain a separate notification system for primary receivers.

At the request of the Department of Justice, the National Center for Missing & Exploited Children (NCMEC) created a system whereby AMBER Alerts can be sent to private companies and vendors across the country. This in turn redistributes the alert to customers who have signed up to receive them. The alerts must be targeted to customers within the alert's geographic area, as directed by law enforcement.

When an AMBER Alert Coordinator activates an AMBER Alert, it must be sent immediately to primary distributors such as radio stations, television stations, and transportation road signs. Coordinators are also asked to send the message to NCMEC, who will configure the message for secondary distribution and send it (via an XML feed) to all distributors who have submitted an operational plan outlining services that can be provided and have signed a memorandum of understanding with NCMEC. This process occurs regardless of the technology format that each Coordinator uses. The secondary distributor then immediately redistributes the alert to its customers in the specified geographic area. Any updates and cancellations will be distributed the same way. Each vendor enters into an agreement in which it cannot charge law enforcement or the public for these alerts. Currently, the program includes Internet service providers and social networking Web sites (AOL, AIM, MSN, Yahoo, MySpace, and Facebook), the trucking industry through Qualcomm, Wireless AMBER Alerts, Digital Billboards, and some members of the hotel industry.

More information about AMBER Alert secondary distribution and a list of current secondary distributors can be found at www.amberalert.gov/secondary_distribution.htm.

+ Develop a backup plan so the AMBER Alert will be disseminated even if the Web site is down.

+ Clarify ownership and responsibilities of the Web site application with the service provider through a service level agreement.

+ Have a process in place to build security into the entire Web site application.

+ Scan the application and review the source code prior to deployment and during production.

+ Develop and implement regular monthly or quarterly security scans of the application.

Marketing

It is important not only for law enforcement agencies but for the public in general to be aware of the criteria for activating AMBER Alerts. The AMBER Alert Program depends on the public's participation to make it effective in the recovery of abducted children. To maintain the public's interest, they must understand that their participation is critical to the safety of children. The media are partners in this endeavor and can assist in communicating the criteria when criticisms occur or activations are denied.

Coordinators have used the following ideas to market their local programs successfully:

+ Publish information about the AMBER Alert Program on the agency's Web site and ask partner agencies to link to the site.

  • Active AMBER Alerts should be posted prominently on the Web site and should include information about how to report tips.

  • Consider posting a frequently asked questions page on the Web site.

+ Recognize National AMBER Alert Awareness Day and get the media involved.

+ Several states have partnerships with the state lottery commission for distribution of alerts via lottery tickets.

+ New York sends alerts to taxicabs and limousines to be displayed on televisions within the vehicles.

Several states have developed public service announcements, brochures, and other videos and publications that help market and publicize the AMBER Alert Program. These marketing tools are usually available to other Coordinators and programs on request.

Issuing an Alert

Some plans require the Coordinator or his or her designee to be part of the approval process when an alert is requested. Most plans require the Coordinator to make the decision if a request is made to activate an alert from another state or a jurisdiction not included in the plan to ensure that the activating state or jurisdiction's criteria are met. When issuing an AMBER Alert, some state plans have a mechanism to activate the Emergency Alert System (EAS) and messaging signs in targeted areas based on information as to where the abductor may be and the time the child went missing. (The alert can be updated as the information changes.) In all cases, the decision to activate should be based on a checklist of actions that the law enforcement agency took to ensure that the child could not be located and the criteria for activation were met. The plan should require that the agency requesting the alert has an investigative point of contact available in case any followup issues or questions arise. This is especially important when the alert is issued after normal business hours.

In Florida, a three-way call is held between the state clearinghouse that issues the alert, the on-call special agent supervisor in the region where the child went missing, and the agency detective handling the case. The purpose of the call is two-fold: first, to ensure that the case meets the criteria for an AMBER Alert and that information about the child and the abduction was entered into the

National Crime Information Center and second, to make sure all available resources are provided to the agency. For each alert, a Florida Department of Law Enforcement agent is dispatched to the agency to liaison with the state clearinghouse and to provide all available state resources, the agency is offered the resources of the regional Child Abduction Response Team, the sex offender registry is made available, and the social service agency databases are checked for any information that could be relevant to the case investigation and to eliminate the parents as suspects.

The following are additional tips from other practitioners:

+ Establish protocols for when an alert is activated, such as notifying the missing children clearinghouse and Child Abduction Response Teams, and using other investigative tools as part of the response.

+ Consider developing uniform scripts for the notifications that are part of the activation, such as scripts for the media, the state department of transportation (DOT), and the state lottery.

+ Have a communications plan in place. One spokesperson should be available to speak with the media and all state agencies and partners.

+ Have a script prepared for individuals who the media may contact that directs them to the single point of contact.

+ Monitor alerts that air on television and radio stations and those that are disseminated via pagers, cell phones, and e-mail.

+ Document the information that the agency provided to justify the request for use in an after-action review.

+ Notify television and radio stations, DOT, and EAS providers of an impending alert so they will be ready when the alert is activated.

+ Offer assistance to the initiating law enforcement agency.

+ When a vehicle and license plate number are used in an alert, query the tag number to see if it matches the vehicle and verify with the local agency if there are any discrepancies.

+ Hold a daily internal briefing or conference call to help control the message and keep information consistent.

Endangered Missing Advisory

Several states have enacted an Endangered Missing Advisory (EMA) plan that can be used when the AMBER Alert criteria are not met but a missing child is considered to be endangered. These alerts gain the media's attention and publicize the case without the risk of overusing the Emergency Broadcast System or variable message signs. EMAs are an important additional tool in cases involving missing children; read more about EMAs in *Guide for Implementing or Enhancing an Endangered Missing Advisory,* www.ncjrs.gov/pdffiles1/ojjdp/232001.pdf.

Convening an Oversight Committee

Oversight committees have proven to be an important part of the AMBER Alert Program at the state, regional, and local levels. Oversight committees typically include law enforcement agencies, E–911 centers, state DOTs, and the media. Although the composition of the committee should be flexible and should reflect the unique mixture of each individual plan, each committee should—

+ Review each AMBER Alert incident to determine if the circumstances merited activation.

+ Review and critique the process used to activate the alert and identify any problems that should be addressed.

Other responsibilities may include processing requests for special training, making changes to the plan, providing a forum for discussing other issues that may arise, and keeping stakeholders informed about any concerns.

The committee should be formal, with a designated person to schedule meetings, ensure that minutes are kept, and compile periodic reports. The committee could elect a chairperson for that role or the Coordinator can serve as the designee.

Evaluating Activations and Conducting After-Action Reviews

The Coordinator evaluates activations to make sure that decisions were made appropriately and activation steps were followed. Each review should either result in affirmation of current policies and procedures or changes that address gaps, enhance the program, or identify any training needs for local agencies or AMBER Alert partners.

The Coordinator also defends the program's guidelines and criteria when an alert is not activated. This can be particularly difficult when circumstances do not indicate that an alert should be activated, but subsequent information and an investigation reveal that a child was abducted. A well-defined and established program that operates with strong partnerships will withstand these situations, which can often be emotional and difficult depending on the outcome of the case.

The oversight committee can be the vehicle for the Coordinator to conduct after-action reviews of all requests for AMBER Alerts to ensure they were handled appropriately according to the criteria and guidelines established in the MOU. This process should be viewed not as criticism, but rather as a means of improving the AMBER Alert system. Specifically, these reviews should include the following:

✦ **Review of denial for an AMBER Alert.** Reviewing AMBER Alert denials is just as important as reviewing activations. Not all instances of a missing or abducted child will meet AMBER Alert criteria. However, even if a case does not qualify, law enforcement agencies should use other resources and strategies to safely recover a missing child. Part of the review

process should be to determine what other resources were suggested or provided to the agency.

When an alert is denied, all available information about the incident that was considered in the decisionmaking process should be documented. The process should be standardized and should include a review of the incident, decisionmaking points, reasons for denial, and other actions that were taken to safely rescue the child. Any denials made in error should be reviewed and suggestions for improvements discussed. If too many requests for activation are not meeting AMBER Alert criteria, stakeholders should consider providing more training to law enforcement.

✦ **Validation of AMBER Alert activations.** To maintain consistency and program integrity, all available information relating to AMBER Alert activations should be documented in a standardized format. The AMBER Alert Coordinator should share this information with the after-action review committee via a formal process. Reviews should be timely and ongoing and should not interfere with child recovery efforts. The review focuses on the information available at the time of the activation, not the final outcome; therefore, suggestions for improvement may result even if the activation was carried out without any problems. The team should not only review the decision to activate but the activation process itself, such as the time it took to issue the alert and any issues that recipients of the message reported.

Practitioners recommend that when conducting an after-action review, the AMBER Alert Coordinator should—

✦ Examine the composition of the review committee and consider expanding it to include a member of the broadcast community, nonprofit organizations, media representatives, and other stakeholders and partners if they are not already included.

+ Ask the initiating agency to provide an incident report and arrange a meeting time so everyone involved in the alert can participate in the review.

+ Present a timeline that includes the time the initial call was received; decisions that were made to issue the alert; when the alert was received on cell phones and highway signs; and when the alert appeared on television stations, radio stations, and Web sites.

+ Create a master timeline that incorporates input from all involved partners. The Coordinator should also create a list of issues to consider, including questions about the AMBER Alert criteria and technical or communication problems.

Chapter 8. How To Improve an Existing AMBER Alert System

This chapter describes additional ways in which a region or state can enhance its AMBER Alert Program.

Interstate Networking

With the rapid nationwide expansion of the AMBER Alert system, Coordinators must maintain a network of communication to ensure that the system is orderly and seamless. Child abductors do not recognize geographic boundaries, and interstate child abductions underscore the need for AMBER Alert Coordinators to work with their counterparts in other states and communities. Ongoing communication and collaboration are vital parts of this process. Several children have been recovered due to the cooperation of states in a multistate activation. In some cases, as many as four states in close proximity activated their alert because of information that indicated the suspect may be in their jurisdiction.

Community Awareness Strategies

One of the most challenging tasks that the AMBER Alert Program faces is increasing the public's awareness of the AMBER Alert plan and the dangers of child abduction. Many people believe that AMBER Alerts are issued every time a child is missing, regardless of the circumstances, and they are not always aware that the AMBER Alert is only one of many tools that law enforcement can use when a child is missing or in danger. In addition, parents and caregivers may not have the valuable information they need to prevent a child abduction and to aid in the child's recovery. Thus, an important task is to give constant, consistent reminders to parents and children about preventing abductions and the tools that are available when a child is missing.

The public should also be assured that any attempts by an individual to falsify a report that results in an AMBER Alert being issued and resources being expended will result in prosecution of the person making the report and possible civil remedies for expenses incurred or revenue lost. Publications, public service announcements, seminars, and forums are effective vehicles that can be used to increase public awareness of the AMBER Alert plan. AMBER Alert partners, including the media, state departments of transportation, and state missing children clearinghouses, can and should be called on to help get the message out to parents, children, and the public.

The National Center for Missing & Exploited Children's (NCMEC's) Web site (www.missingkids.com) offers a number of publications and other resources (under the "Resources for" category, click on "Parents & Guardians" and "Law Enforcement"). In addition, every state has a missing child clearinghouse that provides resources and services for missing children, their families, and the professionals who serve them. The contact information for each clearinghouse can be accessed on NCMEC's Web site (www.missingkids.com/lawenforcement). Click on "Missing-Child Clearinghouse Program" under "Featured Services."

Training

The process for developing and implementing an AMBER Alert plan is complex. The issues surrounding missing children are equally complex. Appropriate training that addresses these complexities must be provided. A systems approach to developing training should be followed; this will help to clearly define the knowledge, skills, and abilities that AMBER Alert partners need to be effective in the child recovery process.

Although many law enforcement officers and investigators will never encounter a child abduction or an AMBER Alert, those who have experienced these types of cases are usually not prepared for the immediate surge of media attention, the impact on their community, the strain on agency resources, and other dynamics that occur as part of the search and investigation. Therefore, training is critical. Training scenarios and tabletop exercises are strongly recommended to help an agency prepare for a child abduction event.

A formal training needs assessment for AMBER Alert should be completed annually. The major components of the planning and development process should include the following:

+ **Establishment of an AMBER Alert training committee**. State and regional programs should form a workgroup to collect information on training needs and determine how to address these needs. In local plans, a committee responsible for oversight or quality control could play this role.

+ **Assessment of AMBER Alert activations**. This information should be collected as part of the incident review process that addresses the strengths and weaknesses of AMBER Alert plans. Training needs should also be addressed as part of this process. The assessment report should include tables that

list each topic, the priority that should be assigned to each topic, the knowledge and skills needed, the target audience, and the potential source of training for each topic.

+ **Needs assessment surveys**. These surveys should identify specific problems or topics to assess the types of training required. The surveys should ask questions about the training method to be used and the depth of training required.

Adequate preparation and delivery are important when planning to conduct training sessions. Because child abduction investigations are time sensitive, training should not be haphazard or be viewed as on-the-job training. Instead, it must be ongoing, thorough, and detailed enough to meet the demands of an unfolding child abduction investigation. First responders, supervisors, investigators, and command-level personnel must clearly understand their responsibilities.

Ongoing training and technical assistance regarding missing and abducted children are available through the AMBER Alert Program. For more information, visit www.amber-net.org.

Chapter 9. Additional Resources

Following are resources relating to AMBER Alerts.

Department of Justice AMBER Alert Web site

A central repository of AMBER Alert resources, the Web site provides a brief history of the program, links to state contacts and AMBER Alert plans, press releases, publications, and guidelines.

www.amberalert.gov

Office of Juvenile Justice and Delinquency Prevention

The Office of Juvenile Justice and Delinquency Prevention (OJJDP), a component of the Office of Justice Programs, U.S. Department of Justice, promotes effective policies and procedures to address the problems of abused, neglected, missing, and exploited children. OJJDP also administers programs related to crimes against children and provides leadership and funding in the areas of enforcement, intervention, and prevention.

www.ojjdp.gov

AMBER Alert Training and Technical Assistance Program

The Department of Justice's AMBER Alert Training and Technical Assistance Program provides technical assistance training and services to federal, state, local, and tribal law enforcement agencies as well as other key AMBER Alert stakeholders to increase collaboration, improve skills, and develop effective policies and practices to protect and safely recover missing, endangered,

and abducted children. An Internet-based collaboration portal has been developed to facilitate distance learning, opportunities, discussion boards, and secure avenues for partners to share protocols, videos, and publications.

www.amber-net.org

www.NCJTC.org

Federal Bureau of Investigation

The Federal Bureau of Investigation (FBI) offers the following resources for investigations of missing children:

✦ Crimes Against Children Program

  www.fbi.gov/about-us/investigate/vc_majorthefts/cac

✦ FBI Tips and Public Leads

  https://tips.fbi.gov

National Center for Missing & Exploited Children

The National Center for Missing & Exploited Children (NCMEC) is a nonprofit organization that works in cooperation with the Office of Juvenile Justice and Delinquency Prevention. NCMEC serves as a clearinghouse for information on missing and exploited children, provides technical assistance to law enforcement agencies and members of the public, offers training programs to law enforcement and social service professionals, distributes photographs and descriptions of missing children worldwide, creates and coordinates child protection education and prevention programs and publications, coordinates child protection efforts with the private sector, networks with nonprofit service providers and state clearinghouses on cases involving missing children, and provides information on effective legislation to help ensure the protection of children. Congress established NCMEC in 1984, and since that time, it has operated a toll-free 24-hour national missing children's hotline, assisted law enforcement in the recovery of more than 100,000 children, and established a CyberTipline that receives reports of child sexual exploitation and a Child Victim Identification Program that reviews and analyzes child pornography images and videos.

Team Adam. NCMEC's Team Adam program rapidly deploys experienced, retired federal, state, and local investigators to the scene of endangered missing children and provides onsite resources to law enforcement and the victim's family. These investigators are selected through a formal process that involves an evaluation by a committee made up of representatives from federal, state, county, and local law enforcement executives who are experienced in investigations involving crimes against children. Consultants are selected based on their skills and experience in the investigation of violent crimes and crimes against children, command post operation, multijurisdictional cases, victim-witness assistance, search and rescue, crime scene management, and Internet exploitation.

www.missingkids.com; 800–THE–LOST

National Criminal Justice Reference Service

The National Criminal Justice Reference Service is the central repository for government brochures, statistics, and other materials and resources related to criminal justice in the United States and abroad.

www.ncjrs.gov

Association of Missing and Exploited Children's Organizations

The Association of Missing and Exploited Children's Organizations is an organization of member agencies in the United States and Canada dedicated to serving the cause of missing and exploited children, their families, and the community at large.

www.amecoinc.org

Endnotes

1. As recorded by the National Center for Missing & Exploited Children.

2. Public Law 93–415, title IV, § 402, as added by Public Law 98–473, title II, § 660 (Oct. 12, 1984), 98 *Statutes at Large* 2125, as amended; codified at 42 U.S.C. 5771–5780a(2010).

3. 42 U.S.C. 5773(c)(1)(2010).

4. The Washington State Attorney General's Office and the Office of Juvenile Justice and Delinquency Prevention prepared two reports from the Case Management for Missing Children Homicide Investigation study, one in 1997 and the second in 2006. Gregoire, C.O., Hanfland, K.A., Keppel, R.D., and Weis, J.G. 1997. *Case Management for Missing Children Homicide Investigation.* Olympia, WA: Washington State Attorney General's Office and Washington, DC: U.S. Department of Justice, Office of Justice Programs, Office of Juvenile Justice and Delinquency Prevention; and McKenna, R., Brown, K.M., Keppel, R.D., Weis, J.G., and Skeen, M.E. 2006. *Investigative Case Management for Missing Children Homicides: Report II.* Olympia, WA: Washington State Attorney General's Office and Washington, DC: U.S. Department of Justice, Office of Justice Programs, Office of Juvenile Justice and Delinquency Prevention.

5. For a presentation of findings from the NISMART–1 study, see Finkelhor, D., Hotaling, G., and Sedlak, A. 1990. *Missing, Abducted, Runaway, and Thrownaway Children in America—First Report: Numbers and Characteristics, National Incidence Studies.* Washington, DC: U.S. Department of Justice, Office of Justice Programs, Office of Juvenile Justice and Delinquency Prevention.

6. For an overview of the NISMART–2 study and its four components—the National Household Survey of Adult Caretakers, the National Household Survey of Youth (both of which surveyed members of a national probability sample of households regarding missing child episodes), the Law Enforcement Survey (which surveyed law enforcement agencies in a nationally representative sample of jurisdictions about stereotypical kidnappings, defined in note 7 below), and the Juvenile Facilities Study (which surveyed juvenile institutions regarding runaways from those institutions)—see Sedlak, A.J., Finkelhor, D., Hammer, H., and Schultz, D.J. 2002. *National Estimates of Missing Children: An Overview.* Washington, DC: U.S. Department of Justice, Office of Justice Programs, Office of Juvenile Justice and Delinquency Prevention.

NISMART–3, an update of NISMART–2, is underway; results are expected in 2013.

7. A stereotypical kidnapping occurs when a stranger or slight acquaintance perpetrates a non-family abduction in which the child is detained overnight, transported at least 50 miles, held for ransom, abducted with intent to keep the child permanently, or killed. Sedlak, A.J., Finkelhor, D., Hammer, H., and Schultz, D.J. 2002. *National Estimates of Missing Children: An Overview.* Washington, DC: U.S. Department of Justice, Office of Justice Programs, Office of Juvenile Justice and Delinquency Prevention, p. 4.

8. Public Law 108–21, 117 *Statutes at Large* 650–696 (April 30, 2003).

ADDITIONAL RESOURCES

For more information about the AMBER Alert Program,
including training, technical assistance, and laws,
visit the U.S. Department of Justice Web site at:
www.amberalert.gov

To report an emergency situation or to
provide information about a missing or exploited child,
call 911 to notify your local police or call:
800–THE–LOST (800–843–5678)

To report information about child pornography,
child molestation, child prostitution, and the
online enticement of children,
log on to the CyberTipline at:
www.cybertipline.com

For more information on missing and
exploited children, visit the National Center for
Missing & Exploited Children at:
www.missingkids.com

www.ingramcontent.com/pod-product-compliance
Lightning Source LLC
Chambersburg PA
CBHW081613170526
45166CB00009B/2952